COUNT FOUR.

.

Count Four.

POEMS

Keith Kopka

UNIVERSITY OF TAMPA PRESS

Manufactured in the United States of America
Printed on acid-free paper ∞
First Edition

Cover graphic by Scott Ehrhart
Cover design by Joshua Steward

The University of Tampa Press
401 West Kennedy Boulevard
Tampa, FL 33606

ISBN 978-159732-178-5(hbk.)
ISBN 978-159732-185-3 (pbk.)
ISBN 978-159732-180-9 (ebk.)

Browse & order online at
http://utpress.ut.edu

Library of Congress Cataloging-in-Publication Data

Names: Kopka, Keith, author.
Title: Count four : poems / Keith Kopka.
Description: First edition. | Tampa, FL : University of Tampa Press, [2020]
  Identifiers: LCCN 2020019207 (print) | LCCN 2020019208 (ebook) | ISBN
  9781597321785 (hardback ; acid-free paper) | ISBN 9781597321792
  (paperback ; acid-free paper) | ISBN 9781597321808 (ebook)
Subjects: LCGFT: Poetry.
Classification: LCC PS3611.O66 C68 2020 (print) | LCC PS3611.O66 (ebook)
  | DDC 811/.6--dc23
LC record available at https://lccn.loc.gov/2020019207
LC ebook record available at https://lccn.loc.gov/2020019208

Contents

SECTION III

COUNT FOUR.

Interrogation

            Once, I ran a whole length of forest
lifting anything I could manage: bees' nests,
flowers, birds' eggs. I even got
some rocks and used them to kill
a few, minor animals, so I could lift them,
too. I wish you could've seen it:
                a hundred toads balanced
in the mouths of a hundred squirrels.
The squirrels then laid over a whole surfeit
of skunks that I, all by myself, managed
to position, just so, on the backs of no fewer
than ten fisher cats.
             All of it stacked and lifted
so high above my head, you would've been
impressed with how well I lifted. I used
my knees, never my back.
             By then I'd circled all the way around
to my father's house again. Same house I grew up in.
So I ring the doorbell, and when my father answers
I start to name what I've lifted.
             But before I get too far, he narrows

an eye at me, then he spins me around, marches
me back to the woods. My father watches
as I put each bird, stick, bug, and fox, dead or alive,
back where they'd come from. It took what felt like years
to re-stage each item.

                That's how you end up hurt,
lifting with your back. My father taught me that,
and his father taught him.

I

You, Strung

Young John Wayne leaps, without effort,
onto the back of a Palomino, and I know
he'll catch the leader of the Taylor Gang
for what he's done to his woman. He'll swing
for this one. Wayne is ruthless, but it's hard

to forget him cut open for cancer research,
the forty pounds of meat wadded through
his colon like a saddle strap. You and Wayne
have a lot in common: doctors

searched the mineshaft of your stomach,
catalogued what they took, then fastened
you with a wandering stitch. Still, nothing
extracted from anyone can explain why
the interior takes its revenge.

                        ⅲ   ⅲ   ⅲ

Hanging is the ninth most popular
suicide method behind gunshot to the chest;
it has a seventy-eight percent

success rate, and takes seven minutes.
In the West, thousands gathered
to watch hanging judges size bight

and neck, and after the bags dropped,
some took pieces of the scaffold or rope
as keepsakes. You hung, too.

I still have the pair of shoes
you loaned me in gym class on
a nail hook in the back of my closet.

        III   III   III

Wayne and his bounty hunters use a horse
for the hanging under the only Joshua tree
for fifty miles. The outlaw, forced
to straddle it. Then the shot, and I hear
the punch of horseshoes
on clay. The camera steadies itself

on the twitch of boot-heels climbing
in air. There's a clank of spur,

taut twine pops. The halo
of vultures, and the posse flattening
their hats against the sun. They pat

at the necks of their startled horses who wait
for the tug to signal it's time for them
to carry their burdens back to town.

     ııı ııı ııı

Before you, the movies taught me
hanging was the only true option
for justice, and if you didn't
deserve to die, someone
saved you, or the rope snapped,
and near-death experience turned
a decent man to revenge. I've spent hours

researching the techniques
for execution. Being a hangman
was a family profession. They call
your choice *simple suspension:* your own
weight baffled the air. In movies,

nooses are always neat, but I have
trouble sizing a loop with the cord
of the vacuum my mom gave me
for Christmas. I wonder if it took you

as long to learn a better knot.

      iii   iii   iii

Late at night, I lace your shoes and go out on my deck.
Lack of sleep impairs judgment. The Duke

suffered for years, but there's no sign of it
in the final scene when he loosens his neckerchief,

snaps his horse into a gallop.

      iii   iii   iii

What gave you the guts
to stack bags of shingles beneath
the crossbeam of your parents' deck?

I imagine the fire ants that nest between
the hot tar sheets pouring out to crawl

your ankles. As you pulled the rope tight
in the lily heat, did you swat at them,

or just step off?

Cold Pastoral

I've always dreamed of climbing
behind the wheel of a Zamboni,

choreographing its smooth concentric ballet,
as the augured ice spins into its dump tank.

Though I know, no matter my effort,
kids would sharpen their skates on the sideline,

blades ready again to score my perfected
rink. But don't we all want jurisdiction

over what refuses to be mastered?
Consider the single clematis vine zigzagging

the border wall in a meadow, how it fakes
its own death during a full season's snowfall.

Which leads me to dream number two,
where I am a war re-enactor: Union Soldier

Number Five, blue mosquito charging
bayonet first into Confederate flash,

uncanny, pretending to die
with such precision! Though

I have no real intention
to ever helm the wheel of a dignified

ice chewer, or feign death
over a sunny fence, my impotent muzzle

sunk into the mud. I've trampled
and practiced. I've learned

I need only to be efficient enough
to keep you tolerating the time it takes me

to reload, or to slick a cold, fresh surface
before we're given a chance

to carve it up again.

Asia Carrera's XXX
Butt-kicking Homepage, 1998

Asia is a sexual astronaut,
surrounded by a radiated halo,
a solar system of pleasure
choices, links
to videos, and a chat room.
I am of the first generation
to have sex so quickly
delivered in terms distant
enough from truth, that I'm
still skeptical of pleasure
outside of my body's impulse.

I click on "Pic of the Week,"
and watch her torso develop
down the screen in small jolts
like the unpredictable drop
of a caught Venetian blind. Asia's legs
appear open, window wide,
and I am the morning

spread across her sheets
as she reveals a hoop
pierced through her labia. She holds
a whip out to the camera,
but I'm focused on the manicured
hair pointing down to where
instinct says I lack understanding.

I drift the mouse around her
middle in the same circles
a football analyst uses
to highlight the bubble screen,
or blown pass protection.
I have never wanted more
than I did in that first moment,
her sex un-pixilated. This is
the lie I continue to tell:
her eyes, her mouth, they are open.
She is looking at me.

At the Haunted Doll Market

http://haunteddollsforsale.com/

They call buying them adoption.
The seller knows Betty doll drowned
in a lake because she told him
through his radio scanner, said the words
water, Robert, boat, tree, under, and her name.

Sometimes I listen to my downstairs neighbor
beat his girlfriend. He did twenty-four
years before the state admitted
he was wrongly incarcerated. Pretty sure
I'm not scared of him, but I don't call
the cops either.

Some couples get a doll
because they can't have children,
and each handwritten purchase agreement
begins with a promise that Betty,
or Bianca, would love to join a good
spirit family.

Every morning, my neighbor
helps his daughter up the steep stairs
onto her school bus. Sometimes his girlfriend
comes running to the curb with a book,
or forgotten lunch.

Dresses and new hairstyles
are essential to happiness, reads the tag
on Bianca; Betty's says she's *good with dogs,*
but hates birds. Vendors have
different theories to explain how
a spirit can enter an object.

My neighbor's girlfriend isn't the mother
of his child. I know because
he calls her a *dumb barren cunt.*
In nice weather, all three of them spend
evenings out on their patio. He pumps iron.
She braids his daughter's hair, yells at her
when she won't stay perfectly still.

Monument

Since I've spent
this hour perfecting
a controlled arc
of spray paint to enclose
the giant red "A"
scrawled across
the clapboard siding
of someone's vacation
home, I decide it's
a good idea to run
when the police
appear in response
to the rattan patio
bonfire I've started
with a blowtorch
of hairspray
and lighter stolen
from my mother's
purse; but even though
I fold myself, creep vine
flat along the banks

of the Bristol River,
I am caught, zip-tied
and foot stuffed
into the cubby-holed
backseat of an idling
Crown Vic, my wrists
shredding more with
each strained shout
through the window
at the chubby rookie
left behind to watch me;
even then I knew
he was the boy picked last,
yet secretly too sure
of himself in a body
growing faster than
the small world
it governed. He was
like the dinosaur
sponges I bought
at the market to ripen
in kitchen bowls,
until they capped
their potential by

sucking every
container dry. I swear,
I can see that water
on his cheeks
as he pulls me from
the car by my neck,
getting bigger,
and taller, and thicker
in front of me, my
compliant frame
absorbing each swing
of his nightstick,
until finally I, too,
start to take shape.

Vinny the Tailor

leads my dad and me through the first floor
of the Smith Hill duplex he's sharing with his sister.
She smiles over the edge of her *Soap Opera Digest*,
as we pass on our way to the back-bedroom
Vinny calls the *bambino sezione*.
Minks hang from the ends of the curtain rods,
and on the elbowed wall sconces. I'm here
for my first Easter suit, something to suffer in at church,
and once more at a K-Mart portrait studio.
In the bedroom, Vinny claps my shoulders
like a pair of erasers to size my build, then pulls
a brass buttoned captain's jacket off a lamp.
It fits. I even admit that I like it,
and on the car ride home my dad
makes me rehearse my story:
I got the jacket second hand.
It was outgrown by the son
of someone dad works with.
He has me repeat this back to him
at every stoplight, and by the time
mom asks where we've been, the recitation

begins to feel true as I hear myself
saying it.

    Vinny,
menace of the Jersey
Turnpike, man who never stitched
a thing more complicated
than an alibi, I think of you now
only during the holy trinity
of my suited occasions: weddings,
interviews, & funerals. But I did
love the coat you picked for me. I wore it
until its sleeves unraveled, & then wore it
more.

    I've made my own
kind of bones through years
of silence. But don't think a boy would forget you,
Vinny. How I sensed you behind me a moment
before you draped that coat over my shoulders,
your newly minted Cappo. That bad painting
of canal boats, docked in what I now identify
as Venice, hanging above a bed you'd piled
so high with stolen suits they touched the feet
of the Pardon Crucifix nailed next to it,
just a fraction off center. I remember your sister

called me handsome as I paraded by her
in my new duds; How we both ignored the deal
in progress, my dad haggling our price in the kitchen.

Iki Dugno

Little by little, let's drink a little. Do you love, or do you not?
Or can you not love at all?

–Lithuanian drinking song

Rudy sips his gin,
then unwraps the plastic
around a roll of duct tape

as we tiptoe to the bathroom.
Closing the door, he pulls
long strips; I wait cross-legged
in the tub.

Tomorrow is Christmas. My dad
is asleep upstairs. I am
patient with each piece Rudy sticks
on my outstretched fingers.

III   III   III

My father stands with
Uncle Rudy in the front yard
of a duplex, both

dressed in cowboy hats
and chaps. Rudy's eyes
are half-closed. His arm drapes

around my father's neck
in a loose hug
like a cowhand's bandana.
My dad points a gun
at the camera,
his own father dead
a year.

In his left hand, Rudy
clutches a beer can
against the flat plain
of my father's chest,
its condensation bleeding
into the checkered cloth.

⠀⠀⠀ ⫶ ⠀ ⫶ ⠀ ⫶

When I'm too drunk
to sleep, I stray
through my apartment,

looking for the places
something could enter. A silverfish
skulks the side of the tub.
I make sure the light outside

my front door never goes
dark, and before I can stop
myself I reach down
and close the drain.

⁣⁣⁣   ⁣⁣⁣   ⁣⁣⁣

Each Saturday, when he drove
to the post office, Rudy
measured the trip by how many
beers he could finish,
while my father crawled
the backseat's leather foxhole,
stuffed army men
into the lumbering Cadillac's ashtrays.

⁣⁣⁣   ⁣⁣⁣   ⁣⁣⁣

Rudy died of a heart attack
when I was ten. I remember

his wan body extending
from the half open coffin

like the top of an unwrapped
candy bar, someone's hand pushing
a full glass at me, and
the toast— *Į sveikatą, iki dugno!* —

To health, bottoms up!

      ⁖   ⁖   ⁖

Rudy believed the dead
came to drink
our lives in large gulps
through our toilets
and drains while we slept.

It's Christmas Eve. I'm eight,
and I don't want to die,
so I spread thick layers
of duct tape where I'm told,
and when we get to the kitchen
Rudy lifts me up on the counter,

and I'm tearing tape,
and he's opening the freezer
for more ice, whispering: *Hurry,
please, Keith, hurry.*

        '''   '''   '''

I know I don't drink
like Rudy did. I don't spend
entire days at the Lithuanian Club
bent over a barstool, pickled
eggs and pigs feet suspended
in fluorescence
on both corners of the bar.
I still carry the membership card
Rudy got me as a kid,
when we would spend Saturdays
with the bartender
serving me soda and lime, the string
of blessings before each
sip. When the men raised
their glasses, I followed.

iii   iii   iii

I keep duct tape
in the hall closet of my apartment.
When I get home from the bar,
some nights, I peel strips, but can't bring myself
to stick them anywhere. Instead,
I ball them up, walk out
to the row of cans at the curb.

iii   iii   iii

On Christmas morning, I storm
downstairs to tear through my presents.
My dad is the only one
awake. For a moment,
I wonder if everyone else
is dead. He takes my hand,

and we walk through the house,
peel tape from every crevice,
then stack logs in the fireplace.

We crumple what we've found
into a bouquet of kindling,
sit together on the hearth
waiting for our backs to burn.

Not Holding the Gun

At this cookout,
in a parallel universe,
a version of me lifts
the gun, considers
its weight a handful
of peanuts. But
in this current
rotation of speed
and light, Pak's pump
action is between us
on the table.
The cookout has been
swell, and I'm glad
his sister, my date,
invited me. His mother
is grilling cow tongue.
The whole gang's
here to celebrate
Marshmallow's release
after three years
in Rahway.

He's at the grill
asking for a fourth
helping, the word *Rascal*
carved in his chest
like a pacemaker scar.
In the universe of
wooden nickels,
I am best friends with
this blunt instrument. But
it's not that universe.
My date's brother
is asking
if I'm interested
in a job, simple robbery.
I'd get a part of
the product. He needs
me because it won't
get back to his crew,
or the black gangs,
if a white man robs
his own. I'm the only guy
at the cookout wearing
a shirt. Her brother
has a tattoo of two devils

balanced on the top of
a mountain range.
It covers his whole
stomach. He tells me
if I shoot the guy,
when I rob him,
it's ok. But if I kill,
there's nothing
in this world
he can do to help.
Marshmallow settles
himself in a deck chair,
eyes closed. The meat
on the grill smells like
warm wood. *Hungry*,
I think, is the only word.

Homecoming

No one says a thing the afternoon
my Cousin Danny comes home
for Thanksgiving, dressed in a blouse,

asking us to call him Danielle, the blonde
wig melting down his frightened face
like a slice of processed cheese. When we were kids,
Danny and I saw our dads save a woman

in the street behind Saint Patrick's. She fell
in front of our car, froze like a raccoon
paw deep in garbage, bruises around her
knees. Then a man appeared from a door

and grabbed her pony tail, looped it twice
around his wrist, the way a singer does
with a mic cord. In the kitchen after dinner,
Danielle pulls at her wig, but I remember

Danny's hand, how it turned up the volume on the oldies
station, when our dads jumped from the car,

and the radio blared "Come Go With Me."
Danny and I held hands and sang

every stupid *dom* and every stupid *dooby*
at the top of our lungs until the grim structure
our fathers made raised up before us,
bearing the sag of another man

like an un-staked scarecrow. My aunt dries
dishes while my mother washes.
My uncle rolls his eyes when I toss Danielle
a dish rag, and take my mother's place

at the sink. She gets the hint, fills in
next to me. We work. I feel the whole family
watch. The sink is full of squash and carrot skins.
When Danielle reaches for another plate,

I lace my fingers into hers, and we plunge
them into the clogged basin, together pushing
through whatever remnants are left.

For a Moment I Feel Immortal, or, Rather, Disappointed

No matter what the graffiti on this wall
tells me, I'm positive that Chey

and Rich will not be *2gether*
4ever. But we learn

so much about death when
we're young, its spring held

taut by the suction
of a popup toy, the shock

when it jumps, despite
our anticipation.

When I was six, I held my breath
in the shower and listened

to my mother run the vacuum
until my body collapsed in the tub basin.

I woke in her arms so confident
of my death that when she'd settled me

with a pillow on the couch and returned to work,
I thought, this must be heaven, watching her

maneuver in large circles around the living room.
Chey and Rich might not even be alive right now,

though they declared this wall
a monument to what they thought they'd be.

When I asked my mom if I could get cookies
in heaven, she looked at me as if something

behind my head were talking. *Go get them yourself,*
she said, *they're right where they've always been.*

Georgic on the Boston Comma

Begin with knowing the comma
is a word and the word
is always *fuckin'.* Forget the gerund,
then torque the lazy *u*
into an *a*, and let the vowel
kneel into the roof of your mouth
like a penitent against a church pew.
Now practice placing it in a sentence:
Ma, I stopped on the way, but fuckin'
the spa was out of papers. Notice how
the proper usage places the comma after
the conjunction, or at the start
of a new sentence, as in: *Fuckin' a horse*
cop had traffic stopped all down
Charles starting at Dorchester.
Never use the comma when speaking
to your boss, or to a church figure,
but fuckin' use it as much as you want
on Joan of Arc's feast day,
patron saint of profanity, who once
chastised a soldier for swearing

by reminding him that it's "foolish to sin
when one is so close to death."

But we're all close to death, Joan,
so fuckin' fuck that. This comma, handed
down from generations of working class
parents to their knob-spined
children peddling knock off sunglasses
on beach towels spread out
around the fringes of Jamaica Plain.
Comma that says yes, I believe
in heaven and hell, but I'm too broke
to be scared about it. Comma that admits
there are limits to your dreams
when you live in the same row house
you were born in. Never use the comma
out of anger. Instead, keep it as a prayer,
exalted in syntax. A promise to yourself
that God exists, and fuckin' somewhere out there
he's pretending to listen at least as much
as we're all pretending to talk to him.

Square Dance Conspiracy

Jazz is a Jewish creation. The mush, slush, the sly suggestion, the abandoned sensuousness of sliding notes, are of Jewish origin.
                    −Henry Ford, *Dearborn Independent,* 1921

You preferred the more traditional
steps, a waltz or a quadrille,
what you felt could counteract
the moral decay lurking
in popular music's civil agenda,
while promoting industrial convenience
and the American axiom
of mass production you created:

cheap goods plus high wages
for workers made it possible to sell
the cars you produced right back
to the people who made them.
Not anymore though. Phil Levine
is dead, and there isn't even a day-
labor line for he or his brother
to stand in. Even the music coming out
of Detroit is no good. But you

loved a more wholesome sound, hum
of the factory floor, the fixed time
of an engine. And so you required
employees to attend dances,
events billed as recreation, or a reward
for meeting their deadlines ahead
of schedule. And when that wasn't enough,
you invited two hundred dance
instructors to your mansion in Dearborn
to learn the decorous logic
of the Virginia Reel and the Schottische,
the palsied hop-step behind
the Varsovienne (your favorite).

You funded contests and clubs, bought
ad space in national papers, printed
full-page diagrams of footwork.
Next, you went after the kids,
campaigning to make the Gavotte,
and the Ripple gym class requirements
believing they taught children *social training,*
courtesy, good citizenship, along with
rhythm. You were determined to start a craze,
and it worked. High schools

and colleges added square dance
to their curriculums. Across the country,
dealerships installed speakers,
and invited their customers to events
scored by the Ford Company Orchestra.
Every weekend, in chaste twilight,
couples in prairie-wide dresses and western
string-ties gathered in showrooms,
bowing to each other between the rows
of solemn Model A's while "Whiffletree"
and "Boil Them Cabbage Down"
blared out over closed circuit
radio networks. Today, square dance
is still the state dance of more than half
the states in America. All of this

because of you, Henry, the only American
admired by name in *Mein Kampf*,
captain of industry, who feared jazz
more than another world war. And though
you are long dead, it isn't hard to see your spirit
haunting the picket lines and rallies that sell
their idea of wholesomeness until it reaches
the febrile pitch of hate, your apparition

called down by tiki torch light, or hidden
in the miasma of shadows still polishing
a statue of some confederate general
on horseback, those other men who helped
make this country what it is. Henry,
how at home you'd be with current styles
of choreography; we do-si-do
around each other back to back, returning,
always, to our original positions.

II

Tour

I. On Stage

We look into our audience
like children dressed as ghosts
scaring themselves
in a mirror. You slam
your custom headstock
into a stranger's neck
when he touches the sound
board. Under track lights,
we drip like swimmers.
You chop him down again,
and a tuning peg snaps
off in his shoulder, pokes
through his skin. I think
of the sewing needles
my grandmother left
in the lining of the bedspread
she made me. I keep
playing to the drum machine
while you beat him.

The crowd is so scared
they leave. In every city,
you are my only
friend. We pull the covers
so high above our heads.

II. I Don't Know Where the Gun Came from

We play a house party, and I shoot a hole
in the ceiling.

People believe me

when I say there are more drowning
deaths in Michigan than anywhere else

in the country. The sky is covered
in shell casings. Everywhere fiancées are asleep,

mine in Providence, while I back dive off a roof.
Again, I do not miss her. Though I pretend

she screams for me not to jump,
there's only the thick plash my body makes

hitting ice scabbed over a foot
of snow. I'm lucky

there's only the growing crack

in my phone voice saying, *I need you.*
I'm tired of lies,

my predictable wish to be dragged
back home; what we miss

is a flooded river that cannot dry
its shores until spring.

The current passes.

III. Lafayette, Indiana: Star City

Tonight's designated
front row girl, the sort that yells
loudest for an encore
in each mostly empty room,
appears like some sad
version of magic

during load out. She picks you
to sign her t-shirt. I go down
the block, break bottles

against the birthplace
of Axl Rose, and later,
when your bed squeaks,
hum "Sweet Child o' Mine"
into the nicotine-

stained pillowcase
that is Super 8 hospitality.
There's only two of us
in this band. You keep
reminding me:

no one pays attention
no matter how hard we play.

She's a waitress, no older
than nineteen, mouth caked
in lipstick, pie flour
streaked on her thigh. Watching her,
I can tell by how she keeps
her apron on during sex,
that she'll wait tables forever.

In the morning, she's gone,
our cash is gone, and you
spend an hour locked
in the bathroom demolishing

mirror and toilet. I pour
the rest of last night's liquor
and crank the volume
on the television. Braveheart

screams for his homeland.
Neither of us listens.

IV. Not a Real Movie Cowboy

I tap out two thick lines
on an air-conditioner behind
Katy's Bar and Grill, draw
a Bic from my pocket, whittle

its neck with a knife, and drag
on the metal box top. It's like
watching a hawk skim a waterhole,
forgetting what will claim me
when I die, or how, minutes ago,

I threw up beside a toilet,
listening to the thin sound
of women pissing in the next room.

Don't confuse the pink
mottle of blood in the water
for a sunset. I never had
Manifest Destiny. I have

whiskey, but I don't slide
the glass along a brine-

dusted bar, or believe all the sand
I've ridden through stays
lodged in me like pellet shot,

noiseless skin growing over
that scattered grain. In a dollar-bought hotel,
a girl scales the outcroppings
of my shirt buttons, scans her touch
over the scars. I leave my gun
for the taking on the dresser.

V. With Three Confederate Flags on the Brim

I buy a gas station hat that says *Jesus
Is My Copilot.* I'm wearing it
like a talisman against the smell
of chicken trucks,
and the cannibalistic hill-people
that Northern kids are taught to believe

lurk around every bend. At the counter,
the cashier nods to the bathroom
from inside her plate glass
fishbowl. I take the woodblock key
from the drawer. In the mirror,
my sockets look like coffee-stained
saucers. There's a small
trace of blood on everything
I own. I feel proud. I understand
this country, the bullet holes
in highway signs. My face aches
as I push the blood back in
my head, taste it around
my teeth. In the parking lot,
everything is indecipherably

bright. I hang the key
from the rearview and shift
the van into drive, pretend it's
a stick of dynamite, or a steamroller
pointed straight at the mountains.
My hat is down low.

VI. Kentucky

I've ridden you, kicked the supple flesh
         beneath your hillsides. I haven't slept,
     and through the van window the farms pile onto one another,

each fence intersects, and the shadows of pickets loom
         like caskets for the corralled horses
     to pull along the pastured ground.

Earlier, when the promoter stole our speaker cables, we found him
         in the alley, and claimed,
     we don't want any problems,

but the words meant less with each haymaker
         you rammed into his temple,
     after I locked his arms behind his back.

The show over, someone took a picture of us bleeding
         in front of a Smiths poster.
     We positioned ourselves

like Morrissey and Marr: my head on your shoulder,
         you holding out a handful

of tulips someone passed on stage. We gaze

out toward the camera the way sun
        glints off a vase, or the bit ring
   on a bridle.

VII. Fend

We chain-smoke in a Wal-Mart parking lot, content to leer
      at people through our van windows

as they scare seagulls or change diapers in truck beds.
      The snow gathers in their hair.

During last night's set, I watched the mosh pit consume
      a bouncer. He disappeared under

the scrum of kids until he popped up behind you, grabbed
      your neck, squeezing. *You're done,*

he screamed, babying a palm full of blood,
      where four teeth floated like coffins at sea.

I saved you; pointed at a kid by the fire exit. *It doesn't matter
      who it was*, I say later, *we're already another state away.*

The snow blacks the windows. I chain a fresh smoke,
      stamp the old one on the floor mat. In the dark,

I try to separate the kid from the look I gave you
		that said, *get in the van*. I still hear him crying,

mouth pried open by the hand hooked under
		his hard palate, dragging him to the farthest corner

of the parking lot. *Why us?* you ask. Shopping carts
		crash in their corrals.

Tonight's show is cancelled. We go inside to buy shovels,
		in case we need to dig.

VIII. Notes on Speed

It's always five
in the morning.
We're doing
ninety, or forty,
and in two days
we'll be home. You
say I've got to drive
once we hit
Pennsylvania.
Ten beers in, I don't
want to go back to her,
a girl like a gated community,
where I know I'll quake
all night in her yard,
shove dirt in my mouth,
before I bloom
promises that I'll never
leave again. Committed
to the belief that
she wants the lie
as much as I think
I need to tell it. The sun is

up over the Blue Ridge
Mountains. It's
unremarkable. Just
a ball someone threw.

III

Hiding with My Mom

We know it's coming, its engine
amping like a flooded lawnmower.
We don't board each window,

and we leave the begonias as they are
on the porch. We do deadbolt
the door. In the finished room

above the garage, we drink Pernod
and wait.
           It'll be scarier, you say, *if it knocks.*
           If it knocks that means it has a plan.
I point to the glow emitting
from the roof vent. It's closer now,

and it doesn't sound
like an engine at all. It's more repetitive—
a rattle before quick suction, a thousand
refrigerator doors opening in a round.

Through the window, a streak
of long curls, tentacles against
the glass, lovely as the crest
of a tarpan mare. I pull the blinds.

You begin to sing, gesturing
for me to join you, but I don't
know the words. Your disappointment
hangs its fug like a freshly
snuffed candle.

> *This is your favorite song,* you say,
> *I sang it every night*
> *when you were a baby.*

Embarrassed, I try to follow along,
every syllable behind by just a second
making your echo. When the knock at the door
finally comes, we sing louder,
while the sinks and toilets shake
like each drain holds a stampede
of tiny cattle. The accumulation

of our fear reminds me of when
I was very young, and I hid my medicine
under the rug. I was so sick,
but you couldn't figure out
why I wasn't getting any better.

It knocks and knocks and knocks.

It feels good
being scared with you,

you confess,
And knowing this
makes me want to lay my head
in your lap. Instead,
I clink my glass of Pernod
against yours.

It's just messing with us.
You know that, right?
You nod, asking *Do you have any idea*
why it's so angry?

I don't, I say, afraid

if I tell you the truth
you'll march me right downstairs
to let the damn thing in.

I'll Tell You the Same Thing
I Told the Other Detective

I work for Number One Boss
who buries cars for insurance
money. He throws this
junkyard party, and the Federal
Hill boys show up in convertibles,
sipping anisette. While I bartend,
Number One Boss sits my girlfriend
on his lap. This is my first job.
I'm saving for a car like dad did,
running numbers to woo my mom.
Ferraris, keys in their ignition,
are illegally parked down J Street.
Planting fake tickets and towing
is the bedrock of our business.
Suckers pay to get their cars back,
or we vanish them, split
what's collected. By agreement,
their Ferraris remain untouched.
This is Number One Boss's

number one rule. Dad taught
me how to open a car with
a tennis ball, and the Hill boys bet
I can't. So I pop open one of the big
cicada wing doors on an Enzo,
and Number One Boss cheers louder
than anyone. My girlfriend
giggles at his impression of me
the first time I got arrested: *Please stop,*
you re hurt ing me puh lease, he whines,
pinching out each syllable on her hips.

Coke Folks

are as loyal as any lesser household pet:
          a gerbil or fish whose hunger response
we like to think of as "human"
              when our loneliness projects

itself onto their captivity. Which is why I'm nodding at Judy
          across her kitchen table
crowded with randoms here to score.
              She's cutting a few lines for me

between details of how small her husband's dick is,
          and how terrible the sex has gotten.
He's in earshot, but he doesn't
              seem to notice because

he's getting his back cracked by T.,
          their supplier who, Judy tells me, decided to move in
last week. In a year, Judy ends up
              incarcerated for running over a cyclist

when heading home from Buddy's Oyster Bar.
        But right now she's as in control
as any substitute teacher, yelling at T.
           to put her husband down

because if they keep rocking up
        on each other's backs
one of them is going to kick out the light,
           and no one will be able to see

what they're putting up their noses.
        Just for a moment, our small schoolyard
goes quiet. Then T. slinks away
           to his bedroom, and Judy's husband asks

for a cigarette. Judy says she thinks she's hurt
        T's feelings, and she's going upstairs
to, quote, change into her pajamas. I have a beer
           with her husband, give what cigarettes

I've got to him, and a few other strangers
        who call me *friend* no matter how many times
I offer them my name. An hour into this
           I decide to leave,

but before I'm out the door
            Judy stops me in the foyer
wearing only her panties, slips
                a gram bag into my pocket

she says is just for me, that she's always liked me
            more than her other junkie friends.
She says that we should go out and do this
            bag in my car together. I waffle;

go back into the kitchen for a while and pretend
            to look for the lighter that's still in my pocket.
Judy's not there when I leave again. I worry
            I've hurt her feelings, but only for a moment,

then I drive home to sleep when my body decides
            I'm allowed to. In the morning, I wake
to a pounding at my door, and there's Judy,
            furious, and still mostly naked. She says

she passed out waiting for me, slept the night on the floor
            of my back seat. *Oh my god*, she says,
how could you let me do this? You know everyone's going to be worried
            sick about me. What will they do for breakfast?

After Talking It Over with His Ghost, My Father Tells Me He's Sick

My father's platoon leader broke bricks
with his head, dead man who still appears
to my dad signing patrol signals
in the kitchen. While we cook dinner,
he shouts orders from the yard. I'd grown
tired of the story about the bomb that blew
my father through a wall. Not in any war,
but in Rhode Island where a loaded 9mm
waited in a frozen project furnace
for him to light the pilot. Then his hand
shooting up through the rubble
like in the last pages of a comic book.
But it's this tale that comes to me
when Sean Esafoe gashes my lower lip
with the stock of a squirt gun, and I'm
dragged in the house by my armpits
for fighting. Spitting blood in the sink,
I swear I can hear dad and his lieutenant arguing.
But I'm so proud of taking a hit in the face

I mouth the word *unstoppable*, flex
my muscles in the mirror, while Sean cries
on the kitchen phone with his dad. My father sits
on the tub edge, and folds each piece of
ripped skin back over my knuckles, his lieutenant
staring at me through the window.

Ancient Astronaut Theory

My friends' marriages are failing
in their collective prophecy of a future
where people in love beat the natural
universal order. *But isn't it possible*,
asks the omniscient voiceover,
and I'm thinking, sure,
the pyramids were built by aliens,
Adam and Eve were celestial
beings, and all of us are just
stones paving the road to a Mayan
apocalypse. My friend Don believes
he's good at scratch tickets. I've
seen him scrape a whole stick figure
family off the back windshield of a
minivan. *We are not alone,* the voiceover says, and the debris left by all
the weddings on Earth forms a comet
of hors d'oeuvres and cocktail
napkins barreling through the
coat check room of our singular

universe. Don declares he's never
getting married. He's going to ride
his scratch-off skills all the way
to the state Powerball, buy an RV,
and find the alien settlement of
Branson. I don't believe he'll find it,
so its existence doesn't matter. This
is the circular logic that ignores
your spouse deadbolting the door
when you go out to investigate
the light in the backyard.

Etymology

We need a German word
for when someone you love,
or a celebrity, turns out to be
a scientologist.
                    I know the Germans
have already given us a word for the desire
one feels climbing through a window
to have sex with their first girlfriend
while her father, a floor below, sharpens
his ceremonial Prussian sword,

and another to describe the embarrassment
we feel on our own behalves when our friends'
dance moves look like their most sensitive
parts have been hooked to a car battery,
while an orthodox priest revs the engine.

But the word I propose is more intricate,
acknowledges the choices we make,
while still capturing

the post coital pleasure that comes
when releasing small whiffs of judgment,
                    like when you're driving
and a squirrel darts at your car, so you break hard
just as it turns back to the shoulder,
and you think, *yeah buddy*! *Good call!*
But as you speed up again, the contents shift
in the tiny suitcase of its brain, and it turns
and jumps right under your tire.

The meaning of our word is not in this moment,
but, rather, in what comes after
when you start to admit to yourself that you
might have seen the squirrel starting to turn,
but you couldn't be bothered to break again,

how you feel sad for a second, but then think
you didn't invent the order of species,
and how at this point in history the damn thing
is designed absolutely to die.

So it's unclear whether you're upset
about killing something, or because you've
been trying to find parking for like, twenty minutes,

and now that you finally have,

you're standing at the meter, and it keeps eating

your money without giving you back any time.

Hollywood Ave.

We lived together in that house with no street number, deciding the limits
        of what we could do to ourselves.

The deer came right up to the porch to chew the juniper while we planned
        our futures, frozen pine branches cracking.

     III   III   III

Ian borrowed C.'s truck,
lined up six bullets
in front of his father's grave,
and shoved the barrel
of a Mossberg Bantam
in his mouth. C. got a call
the next morning that the truck
was blocking the cemetery gate.

He asked if I'd take him to get it, and I thought of a woman I'd loved
who believed in ghosts and moved to Bolivia to elude them.

It was a bus accident during the rainy season
that killed her. I often imagine her body

sliced with sunlight and topless, or pouring wildly a thousand feet
per second down the cliffs above the Yungas.

On the phone, the caretaker
said it seemed pointless
to tow the car if we could come
right away, but he warned
it would be gone if we waited.

ııı   ııı   ııı

The streets in our neighborhood were named
after race tracks: Sarasota, Palm Beach, Hollywood Park,
and in the summer, when the tourists bloomed
like sweetgum spines, they brought their dogs
to keep us up all night, and piss our lawn
full of dry brown holes. Ian
and I walked the streets one-night stealing
each street sign, but this didn't cure the people,
or stop their dogs from crying. All summer,
how we wished for tongues much larger
than our own, a desire to sweat the world that contained us.

ııı   ııı   ııı

C. calls me at 2 a.m.
to ask how many cigarettes I smoke
on average, and I know he's judging me.
But I'm in a Chicago parking lot
chaining butts
after spending most of the night
handcuffed to a bench,
and being grilled by a policeman
with a pockmarked face. I remember
throwing up on my car door.
I ask C.
what he means by average,
and I can hear people yelling
in the background. C.
is getting impatient.
Three or four, I say, *but you should see*
how they shave the cell towers into the mountains
of West Virginia, and he says *what,*
and I say *depends on if I've been drinking,*
and C. says *ok,*
and I say *I should get going.*
I have a girl to meet tomorrow,
and I hang up.

⫶ ⫶ ⫶

When C. and I arrive, we see his truck is parked
lengthwise across the graveyard gate.
I make a joke about Ian being dead drunk,
and we're both surprised when the caretaker comes out
to thank us for doing this on such short notice,
during such a difficult time. Behind him, the paths
between the stones are crowded with people
troubling themselves with memory, impatient
to put down the flowers they've been holding.

⫶ ⫶ ⫶

One night in January,
Ian got drunk and shoveled
the driveway while naked. It was the new year's
first snow, and he bent
like a buried elm bough, started close
to the house where the car was,
and lifted small mountains of the heavy wet
like gemstones. He threw
each pile over his shoulder,

his bare body plowing
backward into the street.

All We Do Is Begin

In the morning, when your mother
sets a fresh plate of eggs in front of you,
you say, *thank you,* and spend the afternoon
doing yard work, shirtless in the sun.

Last night, at the show at Lupo's,
you copped a feel off a girl in bondage
pants who floated on outstretched
arms above your head. Palm cupped
around her breast, you were dragged
off. The trick music plays on us all

is that we believe what we feel when
we listen is more than we've already
felt. You followed that girl to an alley
and there, against the piss-coated brick,
she kindly allowed you what you wanted.

Through the wall you heard a song end,
and in its ring the singer counted
to four. You were just starting

to understand how he'd count four
thirty times a night for twenty years.
It is easy to hate what we're given,
especially when it's all we know.

The Birds of Montreal

I reach across the brunette,
pull a napkin from the glove box
so she can blot her lips. I've been
in love with her since we hit
border traffic, the way she smiled
at the Mountie when he asked
why we're visiting. She's a painter,
her husband is a musician, and
they argue in French at the table
like I'm not there. We're eating
poutine in a courtyard canopied
by hackberry trees. At sunset
Montreal looks like the big brick
fireplace I had in Massachusetts,
where one afternoon a tanager
glided down the open flue
and careened around the room
until it broke its neck against
the ceiling. The brunette doesn't
touch her meal, but scoops her
hair behind her ear each time

it blows forward. *The breeze*
comes off the Fleuve Saint-Laurent,
the husband says in his meticulous
accent, before he pays the bill
for everyone. After dinner, we go
to a church basement to watch
him play experimental noise
for a crowd of ten hip shadows,
through a machine that makes
him look like a telephone
operator, while the brunette
and I stand in the corner, close
enough that our shoes touch.
His drone ricochets against
the ceiling and lodges in the base
of my neck. The brunette isn't
paying attention. The show
is a success. We celebrate
at a bar lined in ostrich heads
that peer down at us as if
we're underground. We drink
absinthe, and the husband talks
about the kids who stole a bird
from the wall, how no one ever

caught them, how he imagines
that head in the basement of a frat
with bras and panties looped
around its neck. I nod
to stop from asking him what it is
to be flightless. A waiter lights
my sugar cube. The husband toasts
me, and I tap my glass to his,
stare at the blank in the row
of ostriches. Under the table,
the brunette unfolds a napkin
on my lap, her palm holding me
through the cloth makes a slow,
migratory circuit.

Dwight Yoakam's Hat

*Dwight, you know you look good in that hat . . . you know, I wouldn't
take it off as much as you've been doing lately . . . .*
                                              —Buck Owens

For a moment in the '80s, you were shiny
as an aluminum Christmas tree, your Stetson
a finial ornament, angel on top, an invitation
for us gaze at the beauty below. Now, it's
the hypnotist's pocket watch, a hard bluff
implying the collar matches the cuffs. I observe this
not from a position of disappointment but, rather, respect,
while watching you from the nosebleed section
as your close-up is projected on the billboard-size
TV screens that bookend this stage: Dwight, your hat
is doing its job. Not just on me,

but on the entire crowd who continues to believe it
when you sing about the coal vein of hillbilly music
being the only thing that keeps you *hangin' on,*
the expensive idea that you still break our hearts,
and have your heart broken. Your hat is the linchpin
between nostalgia's illusion and paying twelve bucks
for a margarita at the concession stand. When I'm asked

how I'm doing by a coworker or a waitress, I often
revel in the pleasure of saying: *I feel like Dwight Yoakam
without the hat.* A phrase you've gifted to us in this,
the late incarnation of your beauty, a response
to be grappled with, upending our false-
consensus bias more than balder platitudes like
I'd complain but who'd listen, or *no good deed*

goes unpunished. And I'm convinced there is no one
who understands these epithets more than
you do, as your band leans into the closing number,
and you shuffle forward, grabbing your hat brim
in a two-fingered thank you tug, looking down
at the woman in the front row who's spinning her bra

above her head like a lasso. Beaming out at us,
a hundred feet tall, from the Jumbotron's eight million
light-emitting diodes, who would say you're not worthy
of a hero's sunset adios? You leave the stage,
but we call after you, as if there's a chance you'll decide to stay.

At Dinner, When Someone Says Reading Poems Is Torture

Tell them how the ancient Greeks
invented the Bronze Bull.
The condemned were locked
in its stomach, then a fire under
the statue heated the metal
until they roasted alive. It bucked
while they cooked, and sound
apparatus turned screams
into snorts. Imagine Perillos
of Athens pitching his idea
to the tyrant king, planning
each stage of diabolical casting,
the months taken to chisel
horns and nostrils wide enough
for the perfect amount of agony
to trickle out. When he finished,
Perillos said to the tyrant: *Screams*
will come to you through the pipes
as the tenderest, most pathetic, most

melodious of bellowings. Horrified by
the end of his imaginings, the tyrant
locked Perillos in his own creation,
then fashioned handsome
jewelry from his bones

Acknowledgments

Grateful acknowledgment is made to the following publications in which poems in this collection have previously appeared, some in slightly different versions:

Berfrois: "Coke Folks"; *Cape Cod Poetry Review*: sections "I," "II," "IV," "VII," and "VIII" from "Tour"; *Cincinnati Review*: "Georgic on the Boston Comma"; *Copper Nickel*: "Etymology"; *The Cortland Review*: "Interrogation"; *Evansville Review*: "Cold Pastoral"; *The Journal*: "At the Haunted Doll Market"; *Love's Executive Order:* "Square Dance Conspiracy"; *Mid-American Review*: "Iki Dugno"; *New Ohio Review*: "Not Holding the Gun" and "You, Strung"; *New Orleans Review*: sections "III," "V," and "VI" from "Tour"; *Normal School*: "Hollywood Ave"; *Ninth Letter*: "Homecoming"; *Passages North*: "At Dinner, When Someone Says Reading Poems Is Torture" and "For a Moment I Feel Immortal, or, Rather, Disappointed"; *Southern Indiana Review*: "All We Do Is Begin"; *Tampa Review*: "Dwight Yoakam's Hat," "Hiding with My Mom," "Vinny the Tailor," and "Asia Carrera's XXX Butt-kicking Homepage, 1998"; *Quarter After Eight*: "The Birds of Montreal"; *Queen Mobs Teahouse*: "Monument" and "I'll Tell You the Same Thing I Told the Other Detective."

The poem "For a Moment I Feel Immortal, or, Rather, Disappointed," originally published in *Passages North*, was selected by Cate Marvin for the 2019 *Best New Poets* anthology.

The Poem "You, Strung" was selected by Robert Pinsky as the winner of the 2015 *New Ohio Review* Prize.

First and foremost, I would like to thank Erin Belieu for her friendship, mentorship, love, and guidance. You believed in me and in this book from the very beginning, and, honestly, neither would exist without your unwavering support. Thank you from the bottom of my heart.

I am also grateful to Aerli Austen, Maari Carter, Kim Duff, Kerry James Evans, Bethany Goch, Craig Gogan, Matt Guidon, Chris Hayes, Erin Hoover, Travis Ireland, Adrian Matejka, Chris Mink, Carl Phillips, Jayme Ringleb, and Melinda Wilson, whose editorial guidance, emotional support, unconditional love, and friendship helped this book take shape. Also, thank you to Cate Marvin and Robert Pinsky for selecting my work for recognition.

Thank you to Tim & Rob Condie, Zack Hane, Neil King, Jon & Mike Pagano, Charlie Smith, and all of my bandmates, former or current, for the opportunity to get loud. Steve Vineis, thank you most of all for going to war with me all these years, and for always inspiring me to push myself musically and creatively.

My sincerest gratitude to the entire editorial team at the University of Tampa Press and the *Tampa Review*, especially Richard Mathews, for believing in these poems, for giving this book a home, and for working so diligently to help this collection come to fruition.

Thanks also to Florida State University and its community of writers, as well as the MFA program at the University of North Carolina Wilmington, the Vermont Studio Center, the Port Townsend Writers Conference, and the Chautauqua Institution for providing me with supportive environments to write many of the poems in this book.

Finally, thank you to Dean Gattone, Maureen and David Moorehouse, Donna Rusillo, and my entire family, especially my mother and father, Lynn Gattone and Joe Kopka, for always loving and supporting me unconditionally. You are the reason.

.

About the Author

Born and raised in Providence, Rhode Island, Keith Kopka spent many years playing in and touring with punk and hardcore bands all over the country. His poetry and criticism have recently appeared in *Best New Poets, Mid-American Review, New Ohio Review, Berfrois, Ninth Letter, The International Journal of The Book,* and many others. Formerly the Managing Director of the creative writing program at Florida State University, he is also the author of the critical text, *Asking a Shadow to Dance: An Introduction to the Practice of Poetry* (Great River Learning, 2018), and the recipient of the International Award for Excellence from the Books, Publishing, & Libraries Research Network. Kopka is a Senior Editor at *Narrative Magazine,* the Director of Operations for Writers Resist, and an Assistant Professor at Holy Family University in Philadelphia.

About the Book

Count Four. is set in Garamond Premier Pro digital fonts, based on original metal types by Claude Garamond and Robert Granjon that were designed and cast in Paris, France, in the sixteenth century. The book was designed and typeset by Richard Mathews at the University of Tampa Press.

Made in the USA
Middletown, DE
18 April 2021